JUPITER

BARBRA PENNE

Britannica
Educational Publishing

IN ASSOCIATION WITH

ROSEN
EDUCATIONAL SERVICES

Published in 2017 by Britannica Educational Publishing (a trademark of Encyclopædia Britannica, Inc.) in association with The Rosen Publishing Group, Inc.
29 East 21st Street, New York, NY 10010

Distributed exclusively by Rosen Publishing.
To see additional Britannica Educational Publishing titles, go to rosenpublishing.com.

First Edition

Britannica Educational Publishing
J.E. Luebering: Executive Director, Core Editorial
Mary Rose McCudden: Editor, Britannica Student Encyclopedia

Rosen Publishing
Amelie von Zumbusch: Editor
Nelson Sá: Art Director
Michael Moy: Designer
Cindy Reiman: Photography Manager

Library of Congress Cataloging-in-Publication Data

Names: Penne, Barbra, author.
Title: Jupiter / Barbra Penne.
Description: New York : Britannica Educational Publishing in association with Rosen Educational Services, 2017. | Series: Planetary exploration | Audience: Grades 1 to 4. | Includes bibliographical references and index.
Identifiers: LCCN 2016024211| ISBN 9781508104155 (library bound : alk. paper) | ISBN 9781508104162 (pbk. : alk. paper) | ISBN 9781508103073 (6-pack : alk. paper)
Subjects: LCSH: Jupiter (Planet)—Juvenile literature.
Classification: LCC QB661 .P45 2017 | DDC 523.45—dc23
LC record available at https://lccn.loc.gov/2016024211

Manufactured in China

Photo credits: Cover manjik/Shutterstock.com (Jupiter); cover and interior pages background nienora/Shutterstock.com; pp. 4, 5, 7, 9, 16 NASA; p. 6 Alinari/Art Resource, New York; p. 8 Encyclopædia Britannica, Inc.; p. 10 Photo NASA/JPL/Caltech (NASA photo # PIA00857); pp. 11, 12 Mark Garlick/Science Source; pp. 13, 26 Universal History Archive/Universal Images Group/Getty Images; p. 14 NASA/JPL/University of Arizona; pp. 15, 18, 21, 22, 27, 29 NASA/JPL; p. 17 Photo AURA/STScI/NASA/JPL (NASA photo # PIA01254, STScI-PRC98- 04); p. 19 NASA/JPL/Caltech (NASA photo # PIA01627); p. 20 NASA/JPL/Caltech; p. 23 NASA/JPL/German Aerospace Center; p. 24 Science Source/Getty Images; p. 25 NASA/Handout/Archive Photos/Getty Images; p. 28 NASA/JPL/California Institute of Technology.

CONTENTS

MEET JUPITER

Our solar system is made up of the sun and everything that orbits, or circles around, it. Other than the sun, the largest bodies of the solar system are eight **planets** (including our planet, Earth). Our solar system also includes smaller objects, such as dwarf planets, asteroids, comets, and moons.

Counting out from the sun, Jupiter is the fifth of the eight planets. (Earth is the third.) Jupiter is more than five times farther from the sun than Earth is. Jupiter is also

You can see Jupiter's colorful stripes in this image of the planet, which was taken by the Voyager 1 spacecraft on January 9, 1979.

Planets are large, round bodies that orbit, or travel around, stars. Unlike smaller objects that orbit stars, a planet is so massive that its gravity clears the path it follows by pulling objects toward itself.

the largest planet in the solar system. Jupiter is so big that all the other planets put together would fit inside of it.

Jupiter is one of the brightest objects in the night sky. Through a telescope, people on Earth can see Jupiter's colorful stripes. Unlike Earth, Jupiter has no solid ground. It is made up of gases and liquids.

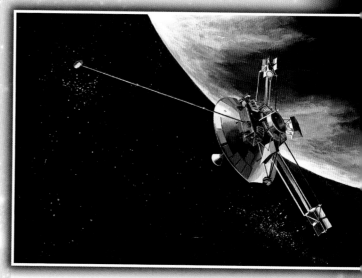

Scientists have sent several missions to learn about the planet Jupiter. Pioneer 10, seen in this drawing, became the first to pass near Jupiter, in 1973.

THE BIGGEST PLANET

The Romans believed that Jupiter ruled from the heavens and controlled the weather.

Jupiter is named after the ruler of the ancient Roman gods. (The same god was called Zeus by the ancient Greeks.) Jupiter is by far the largest planet in the solar system. Jupiter is so huge that more than 1,300 Earths would fit inside of it! The planet measures about 273,000 miles (439,000 kilometers) around. Its diameter is about 89,000 miles (143,000 km).

Jupiter's mass is also much greater than Earth's. Because of its huge mass, Jupiter has very strong gravity. Its gravity affects other objects in the solar system.

Why do you think Jupiter is named after the ruler of the gods?

It changes the paths of comets. It creates gaps in the main asteroid belt. The belt is a thick ring between the orbits of Mars and Jupiter that contains most of the solar system's asteroids. Astronomers think that, when the solar system was forming, the pull of gravity from the object that became Jupiter prevented the asteroids there from clumping together to form a planet.

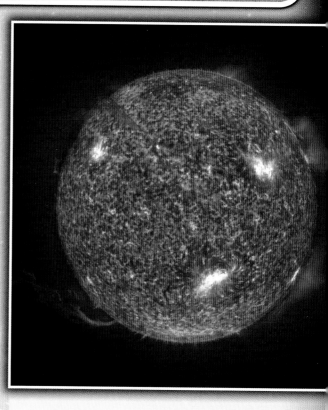

Like the rest of the solar system, Jupiter formed from material that was left over after the sun formed.

A GAS GIANT

The planets in our solar system can be divided into two major groups: the inner planets and the outer planets. The inner planets are closest to the sun. They are Mercury, Venus, Earth, and Mars. These planets are also called the rocky planets. They are made up mostly of rock and metal.

sun
865,000 mi
(1,392,000 km)

Jupiter
89,000 mi
(143,000 km)

Saturn
74,900 mi
(120,600 km)

Neptune
31,000 mi
(50,000 km)

Venus
7,500 mi
(12,100 km)

Mars
4,200 mi
(6,800 km)

Uranus
32,000 mi
(51,000 km)

Mercury
3,000 mi
(4,900 km)

Earth
7,940 mi
(12,780 km)

Sizes given are the approximate diameter of each body.

The four inner planets all have solid surfaces.

Jupiter is an outer planet. The outer planets—which also include Saturn, Uranus, and

Mercury, Venus, Earth, and Mars are rocky planets. They are closer to the sun than Jupiter, Saturn, Uranus, and Neptune, which are the gas giant planets.

In what ways are the inner and outer planets similar? In what ways are they different?

Neptune—do not have solid surfaces. They are made up of gases. They are often called the gas giants. Along with gases, Uranus and Neptune also contain ice and rock. Some of this ice is water ice, like that on Earth. Uranus and Neptune also have ice that is frozen ammonia and methane. In addition to being called gas giants, Uranus and Neptune are sometimes called the ice giants.

Unlike Jupiter, our home planet is a rocky planet. Earth is the largest of the solar system's four rocky planets.

The eight planets in the solar system are classified either as terrestrial (which means Earth-like) or as Jovian (which means Jupiter-like). The inner, rocky planets are the terrestrial planets. The outer, gas giants are the Jovian planets.

Jupiter is almost entirely made up of hydrogen and helium. Photographs make Jupiter look like it has a solid surface like Earth's. However, pictures of the planet actually show its layers of clouds. There is no solid surface. The layers of clouds make it difficult for scientists to observe Jupiter's interior. Instead, they must use their knowledge to figure out what lies beneath Jupiter's cloud layers.

Scientists think that inside Jupiter, pressures and temperatures increase greatly

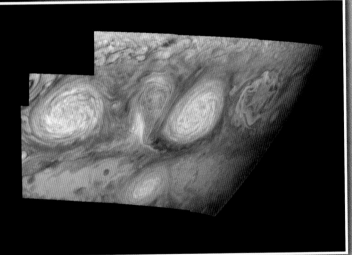

This image of Jupiter's clouds was put together from images taken by the Galileo spacecraft in 1997. The colors were changed to make the clouds easier to see.

with depth. The hydrogen and helium that make up Jupiter become more compact, or denser, toward Jupiter's center. Jupiter's center layer, or core, is made up of hot, thick liquid. There temperatures may reach nearly 45,000° F (25,000° C). The pressure in Jupiter's core is likely fifty to 100 million times the pressure at sea level on Earth.

Jupiter's core is gray in this diagram of the planet's interior. It is most likely made of hydrogen in liquid form.

ORBIT AND SPIN

Like all planets, Jupiter has two types of motion: orbit and spin. Jupiter orbits, or travels around, the sun very slowly. It takes about twelve Earth years for Jupiter to complete one orbit. In other words, a year on Jupiter lasts about twelve Earth years. Jupiter's path around the sun is elliptical, or oval-shaped. Jupiter's average distance from the sun is about 483 million miles (778 million km).

Jupiter spins rapidly. It spins faster than the

This diagram shows the outer planets' orbits. The small objects between Jupiter and the sun are the asteroids of the main belt.

other seven planets. Jupiter takes just less than ten hours to complete one rotation. That is how long a day lasts there. The axis that Jupiter spins around is only slightly tilted in relation to the sun. The sun shines on each part of the planet the same amount throughout the year. For this reason, Jupiter does not have seasons like Earth, Mars, and other planets with tilted axes do.

Jupiter's clouds spin at slightly different rates. The clouds near the equator spin faster than the clouds near the poles.

APPEARANCE AND ATMOSPHERE

Jupiter has a very thick atmosphere. The atmosphere is made up of hydrogen and helium, as well as small amounts of many other gases. When viewed through a telescope, Jupiter appears to have colored stripes and spots. The stripes are bands of clouds, and the spots are large storms. The weather on Jupiter is very stormy. Jupiter's clouds appear in bright and dark stripes that are nearly parallel to the planet's

The darker bands of Jupiter's clouds are called belts, while the brighter bands are called zones.

From 1998 to 2000, scientists observed three small spots in Jupiter's atmosphere combine to form one large spot. Why might this cause scientists to think about how the Great Red Sport formed?

equator. These bands of clouds are pushed around the planet by strong east-west winds. The layers of clouds are also separated by depth. The layers range in color from white to yellow, brown, salmon, and blue-gray. Scientists think that the clouds are different colors because they con-tain different chemicals.

The largest spot on Jupiter is called the Great Red Spot. It is a huge storm that is more than twice as wide as Earth. It was first ob-served from Earth in 1664.

The Great Red Spot is the oval in the upper right part of this photo. The white oval below it is also a storm.

MAGNETIC FIELD

Like most of the planets in the solar system, Jupiter acts like a giant magnet. This is because it has a magnetic field. Jupiter's magnetic field is about 20,000 times stronger than Earth's magnetic field. In fact Jupiter has the largest, strongest magnetic field in the solar system.

Magnetic fields form when electric currents flow through an object. Scientists think that the hydrogen inside Jupiter is under so much pressure from the layers above that it has turned to a liquid metal form. The

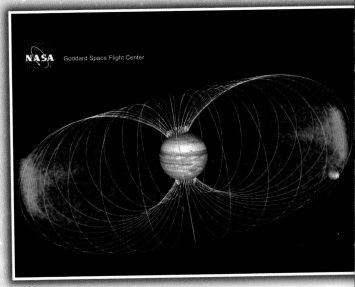

NASA Goddard Space Flight Center

This diagram shows Jupiter's magnetic field. It was made by the National Aeronautics and Space Administration (NASA), which is the U.S. space agency.

Something that conducts electricity allows electricity to flow through it easily.

metallic hydrogen conducts electricity. The flow of electricity through Jupiter's metallic interior forms a strong magnetic field around the planet.

Like Earth's magnetic field, Jupiter's magnetic field has a north pole and a south pole. These are like the poles in a bar magnet. The position of Jupiter's poles is opposite that of Earth's. So a compass would point south on Jupiter instead of north, like it does on Earth.

The interaction of Jupiter's strong magnetic field and its atmosphere causes auroras at the planet's poles, as seen in this image.

JUPITER'S RINGS

All four outer planets have ring systems. Jupiter's system of thin rings was discovered in 1979. Its rings consist of tiny rocks and dust. Jupiter's rings are much smaller and dimmer than the planet Saturn's rings.

Jupiter's main ring is about 4,000 miles (6,400 km) wide and nineteen miles (30 km) thick. Its outer edge is about 80,000 miles (129,000 km) from the planet's center. Between Jupiter and its main ring, there is a

This photo shows Jupiter lit from behind. Jupiter's main ring is yellow, while the planet's outline is red and blue.

Gravity is the force that causes planets to orbit the sun. Gravity also causes particles in the rings around Jupiter to stay in orbit. How are these two examples similar?

cloudlike ring called the halo. Beyond the main ring, there are two outer rings, called gossamer rings. All of Jupiter's rings are made up of particles that were produced when pieces of asteroids, comets, and other objects crashed into Jupiter's moons.

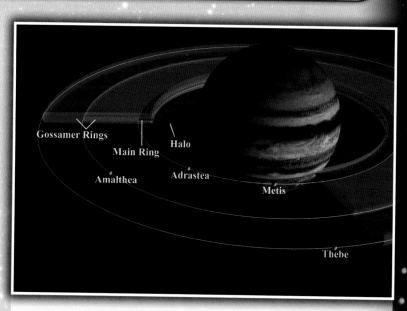

Gossamer Rings
Main Ring
Halo
Amalthea
Adrastea
Metis
Thebe

This illustration shows Jupiter's ring system and inner moons. Scientists think that the rings formed from material from the moons.

JUPITER'S MOONS

Many moons orbit Jupiter. So far, scientists have discovered more than sixty moons. They expect to find even more in the future. Most of Jupiter's moons are small. However, four of its moons are very large. They are called Europa, Io, Callisto, and Ganymede. These four moons are about the size of Earth's moon or even bigger. They were

Jupiter's Galilean moons are, from left to right, Io, Europa, Ganymede, and Callisto. This image shows their size in comparison to each other.

first seen by the scientist Galileo in 1610. Galileo spotted the moons by using a telescope. In his honor these moons are called the Galilean satellites.

In 1892 a scientist named Edward Barnard discovered a fifth moon, called Amalthea, by observing it through a telescope. Scientists later discovered many more moons by examining images taken by telescopes on Earth or by spacecraft. Three of these—Metis, Adrastea, and Thebe—along with Amalthea are Jupiter's four closest moons.

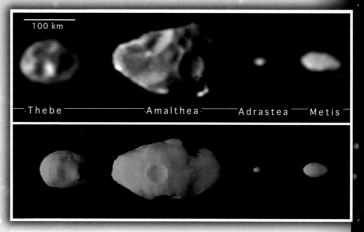

This image is a combination of photographs of Jupiter's inner moons taken by a spacecraft orbiting the planet.

The four Galilean satellites and the four inner moons are called the regular moons. They orbit Jupiter in almost circular paths. They also orbit Jupiter in the same direction that Jupiter spins. Jupiter's other moons are irregular. They orbit on stretched out or tilted paths.

Scientists think the regular moons formed when Jupiter did—about 4.6 billion years ago. They think that as time passed some objects traveled too close to Jupiter and got caught by the planet's gravity. The captured objects became Jupiter's irregular moons.

A huge volcano can be seen on the horizon in this image of Io. Io has the most volcanic activity of any object in the solar system.

Of the four Galilean satellites, Io and Europa are probably rocky, like Earth's moon. Ganymede and Callisto are probably half rock and half ice. The surfaces of Europa, Callisto, and Ganymede are icy.

Callisto's surface has many craters, or round holes that formed when objects crashed into it. Most of the craters are about 4 billion years old.

EXPLORING JUPITER

People have observed Jupiter from Earth since ancient times. Jupiter is one of the brightest objects in the sky. Ancient Egyptian, Babylonian, Chinese, Greek, and Indian astronomers all knew of Jupiter. After telescopes were invented in the 1600s scientists were able to study Jupiter and its moons more closely.

Scientists sent the first **unmanned** spacecraft missions to Jupiter in the 1970s. These spacecraft—named Pioneer 10 and 11

This drawing shows what Pioneer 10 looked like as it traveled through space.

VOCABULARY

An unmanned spacecraft travels with no people on board.

and Voyager 1 and 2—flew by the planet and collected information about it. Both missions sent close-up pictures of Jupiter back to scientists on Earth. This helped scientists discover previously unknown moons of Jupiter as well as other important information about the planet.

Later the unmanned Galileo spacecraft orbited Jupiter. In 1995 it dropped an object called a probe toward the planet. The probe sailed through the upper layers of Jupiter's gases and measured their properties. It was the first man-made object to make contact with a gas giant.

This is an artist's drawing of Galileo passing by one of Jupiter's moons, with Jupiter itself visible in the background.

The Cassini-Huygens spacecraft flew past Jupiter on its way to study Saturn in 2000. It took many new photographs of Jupiter. In 2007 the New Horizons spacecraft flew by Jupiter on its way to study Pluto. New Horizons studied Jupiter's moons and weather. It also detected lightning on Jupiter. It was the first time lightning had ever been observed beyond Earth.

In 2011 a new US space probe named

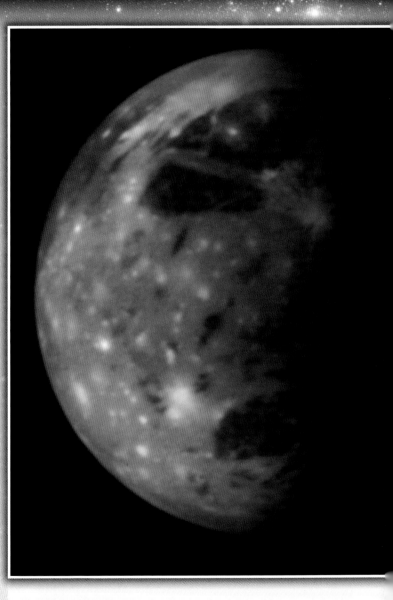

This image of Jupiter's moon Ganymede is a combination of photographs taken by the New Horizons spacecraft.

Why might solar power be a good energy source for spacecraft?

Juno was launched to orbit and study Jupiter. Juno has instruments to study Jupiter's gravity, magnetic field, and atmosphere. It is run on solar power—energy from the sun. In the 2020s the United States plans to send a spacecraft to study Jupiter's moon Europa.

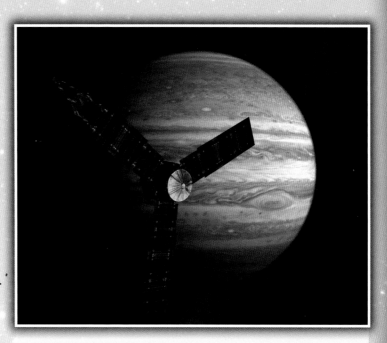

This is an artist's drawing of Juno with Jupiter in the background. The probe began orbiting Jupiter in July 2016.

LIFE ON JUPITER?

Some scientists want to find life on planets other than Earth. Many think that Jupiter's moons may be able to support life. The gases in Jupiter's atmosphere are the same gases that existed on Earth in its earliest years. Experiments on Earth with those gases show that they may be able to create the chemical compounds needed for life as we know it.

Jupiter's moon Europa might be the most likely place to find life. Its surface is icy. Under that ice there may be a salt-water ocean like those

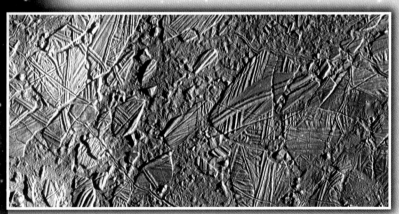

These patterns are cracks on Europa's icy surface. The image was made by combining photographs from the Galileo spacecraft.

of Earth. Ganymede and Callisto also have water ice under their rocky surfaces. With gases similar to those found on Earth, water, and sources of energy, Jupiter and its moons may be the most likely known places for life to survive beyond Earth. In years to come scientists plan to explore Jupiter and its moons more. There are always more discoveries to be made about the gas giant.

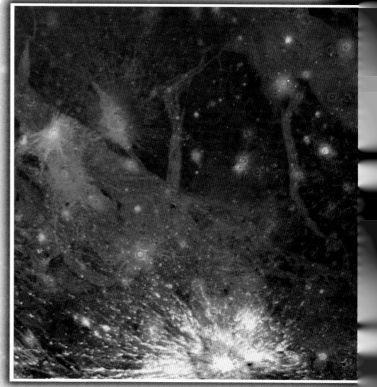

Galileo took this image of Ganymede's icy surface in 1997. Scientists think the lighter areas formed later than the darker ones.

GLOSSARY

ASTEROID One of the thousands of small, rocky bodies between Mars and Jupiter with diameters from a fraction of a mile to nearly 600 miles.

ATMOSPHERE The mass of gases surrounding a planet or other body in space.

AXIS An imaginary straight line around which a planet or other object in space spins.

COMET A small chunk of dust and ice that orbits the sun.

DIAMETER A straight line passing through the center of a circle or sphere.

DWARF PLANET An object in space that orbits the sun and has less mass than a planet, so its gravity is not strong enough to clear other space bodies around its orbit.

EQUATOR An imaginary circle around a planet that is always the same distance from the north pole and the south pole.

GRAVITY A pulling force between any two objects that works across space. The greater the mass of an object, the greater is its force of gravity.

IRREGULAR Not regular.

MAGNETIC FIELD The portion of space near a magnetic body within which magnetic forces can be detected. Magnetic fields also form near objects through which electricity travels.

MASS The amount of matter in an object.

ORBIT To move around another body.

POLE Either end of a planet's axis, or either of the two ends of a magnet.

PRESSURE A measure of the amount of force applied by something to something else in direct contact with it.

ROTATION One complete turn around an axis or center.

SATELLITE A smaller body that revolves around a planet.

SOLAR SYSTEM The sun and everything that orbits the sun. That includes the planets, their moons, asteroids, and comets.

FOR MORE INFORMATION

Books

Adamson, Thomas K. *The Secrets of Jupiter*. North Mankato, MN: Capstone Press, 2016.

Aguilar, David A. *Alien Worlds: Your Guide to Extraterrestrial Life*. Washington, D.C.: National Geographic, 2013.

Cunningham, Greg P. *Journey to Jupiter* (Spotlight on Space Science). New York, NY: PowerKids Press, 2015.

Lock, Peter. *Space Quest: Jump to Jupiter*. New York, NY: DK Publishing, 2015.

Mapua, Jeff. *What Is a Planet?* (Let's Find Out! Space). New York, NY: Britannica Educational Publishing, 2015.

Nagelhout, Ryan. *What Is a Moon?* (Let's Find Out! Space). New York, NY: Britannica Educational Publishing, 2015.

Owen, Ruth. *Jupiter* (Explore Outer Space). New York, NY: Windmill Books, 2014.

Websites

Because of the changing nature of internet links, Rosen Publishing has developed an online list of websites related to the subject of this book. This site is updated regularly. Please use this link to access the list:

http://www.rosenlinks.com/PE/jupi

INDEX